Inktangle 2.0

An inky Pop Icon Hunt
and
Coloring Book

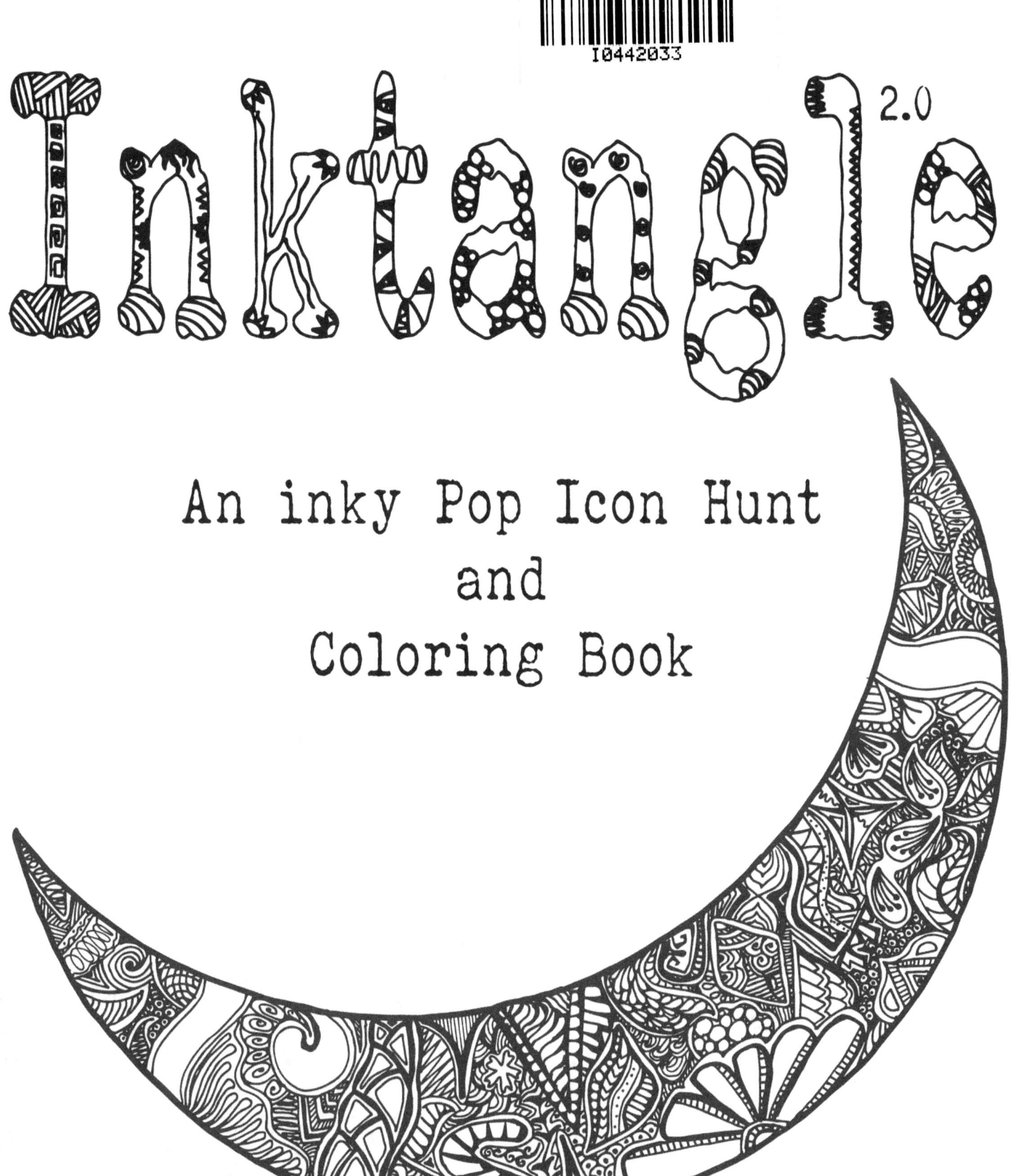

Fahima Aslam

Published in 2016
by Gutter Margin
Appenzell, Switzerland
guttermargin@icloud.com
guttermargin.com

Cover Design: ᕲ. Kali

ISBN: 978 1 52385 104 1

This book
belongs to:

Pop Icon Hunt

INSTRUCTIONS:

1. Find and count all hidden Pop Icons

2. Enter each number above each Pop icon >>>

3. Read upside down ⌣

   Hint: If you cannot find a particular icon, just enter 0.

SOLUTIONS ⊱ at the end of this book

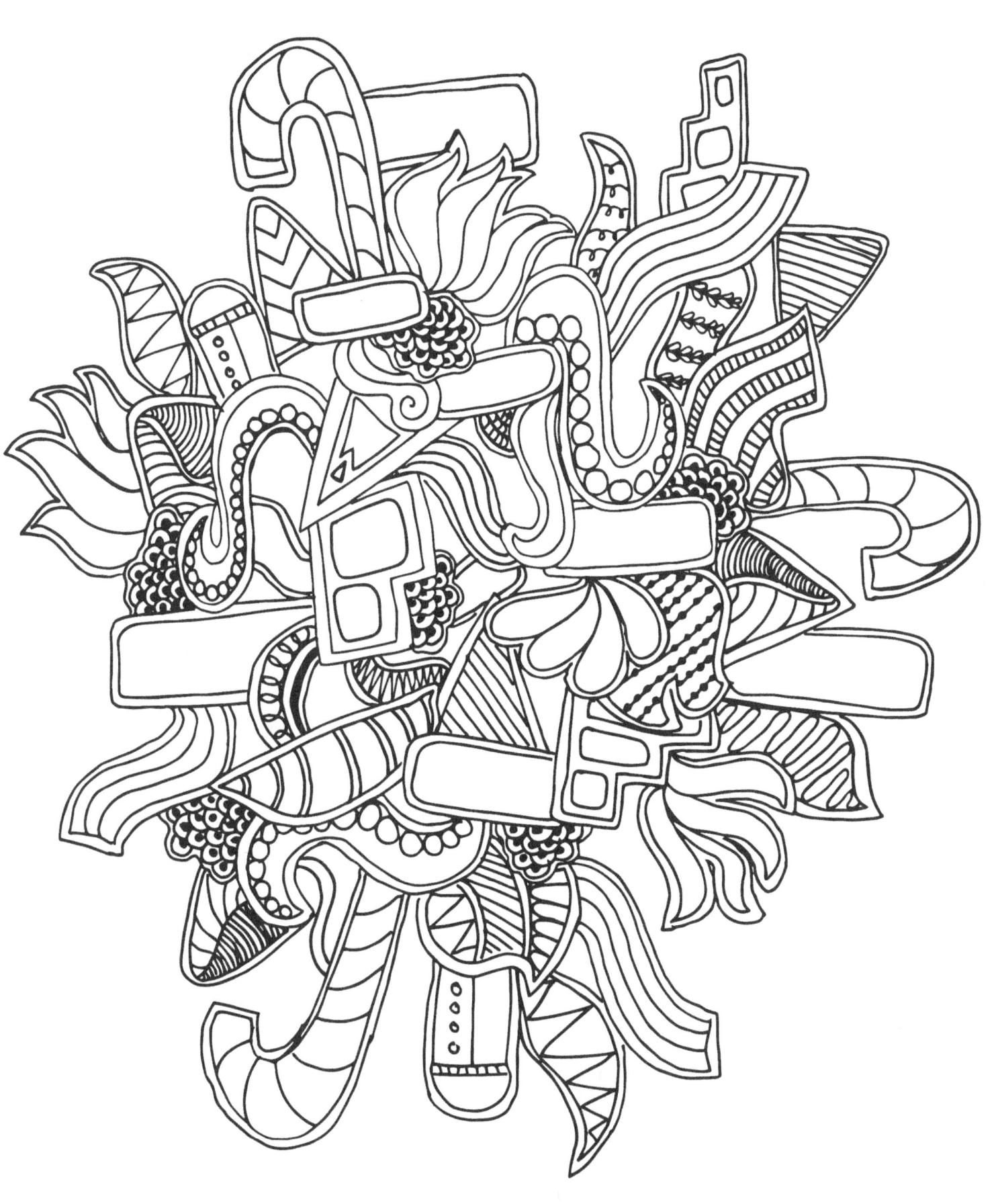

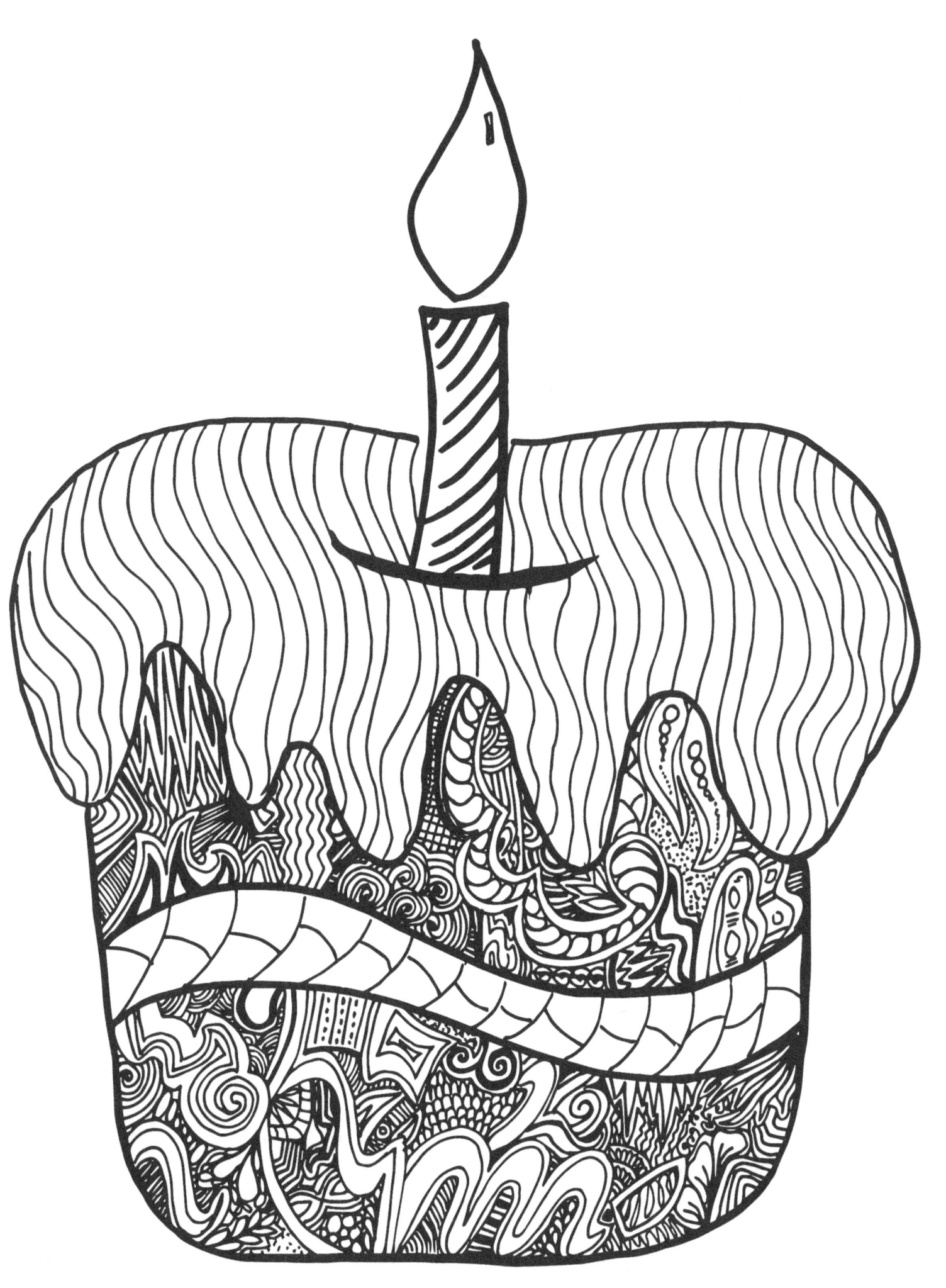

SOLUTIONS

"SSILB SSETOGE"

$$\frac{5}{5} \quad \frac{5}{5} \quad \frac{1}{1} \quad \frac{7}{7} \quad \frac{8}{8} \qquad \frac{5}{5} \quad \frac{5}{5} \quad \frac{3}{3} \quad \frac{7}{7} \quad \frac{0}{0} \quad \frac{9}{9} \quad \frac{3}{3}$$

👽 #1, #6, #8, #19, #28

© #2

☢ #2, #9, #12, #19, #27, #28, #29

📞 #4, #7, #12, #14, #20, #23, #27, #29

☯ #2, #5, #19

📶 #1, #6, #11 (twice), #13, #19, #23, #24, #28

www.ingramcontent.com/pod-product-compliance
Lightning Source LLC
Chambersburg PA
CBHW081357280526
45788CB00009B/2908